·GROWING UP IN·
Ancient Egypt

ROSALIE DAVID

Illustrated by
ANGUS McBRIDE

Troll Associates

Library of Congress Cataloging-in-Publication Data

David, A. Rosalie (Ann Rosalie)
    Growing up in ancient Egypt / by Rosalie David; illustrated by
Angus McBride.
        p.   cm.
    Includes index.
    Summary: Describes daily life in ancient Egypt, discussing life in
the city, life in the country, pets and toys, meals, and other
aspects.
    ISBN 0-8167-2717-1 (lib. bdg.)   ISBN 0-8167-2718-X (pbk.)
    1. Egypt—Social life and customs—To 332 B.C.—Juvenile
literature.   [1. Egypt—Social life and customs—To 332 B.C.]
I. McBride, Angus, ill.   II. Title.
DT61.D3274   1993
932'.01—dc20   91-40264

Published by Troll Associates

© 1994 Eagle Books

Design by James Marks
Edited by Kate Woodhouse

Printed in the U.S.A.

10 9 8 7 6 5

Contents

Ancient Egypt

Egypt, in north Africa, has one of the world's oldest civilizations. Its northern shores lie on the Mediterranean Sea. To the east is the Red Sea. But the most important waterway in Egypt is the Nile River.

The Nile flows from the south into a fan-shaped delta where it meets the Mediterranean. Egypt has very little rainfall, and without the Nile the entire country would be a desert. Before modern dams were built to hold the water back, the river would flood every year, bringing down thick, black mud from the mountains of central Africa and spreading it over the river banks. This fertile mud enabled the early Egyptians to grow plentiful crops. The ancient Egyptians named their country *Kemet*, which meant "black land," because this was the color of the rich soil. The land beyond was called *Deshret*, or "red land."

▶ This girdle of an Egyptian princess is a fine example of the jewelry buried in ancient Egyptian tombs. The pyramids were the tombs of the kings and queens of ancient Egypt. Most of the pyramids are over four thousand years old.

MEDITERRANEAN SEA

Nile Delta

LOWER KINGDOM

SINAI

Giza ●

Memphis ●

Nile River

Valley of the Kings

▶ This map of Egypt shows the land in the Nile Valley and the delta, where the crops were grown, as well as the surrounding desert. Most pyramids were built in the north where these two areas meet.

RED SEA

UPPER KINGDOM

NUBIA

Who were the ancient Egyptians?

People have lived in Egypt for thousands of years.
About 6,000 years ago, people in the Nile Valley
began to develop the way of life we call ancient
Egyptian. They began to build large, mud brick
tombs for their rulers, to make beautiful objects
for their tombs and homes, and to use a kind of
writing. People from Mesopotamia may
have settled in Egypt at this
time, but no one is sure
about this.

▼ The king drove into battle in his chariot, pulled by a pair of horses. He was armed with a bow and a quiver of arrows. Horses were introduced into Egypt in about 1550 B.C.

Two kingdoms gradually developed, one in the north called the "red land" and another in the south known as the "white land." Each had its own king, who wore a special crown. About 5,000 years ago the king of the south conquered the north, and Egypt was united. The king's name was Menes, and he founded Egypt's first capital at Memphis. There were no more wars for hundreds of years.

Cities, towns, and villages

If you visit Egypt today, you can stand with one foot on rich cultivated land and the other in the desert. Thousands of years ago, the cultivated land was kept for growing food and raising animals. People used the desert to bury their dead. The poor people dug shallow graves and covered them with a mound of dirt and stones. The rich people built stone tombs. Stone was also used to build temples. Many of these stone buildings still survive.

Most villages stood along the banks of the Nile. The towns, which were often quite large, were important market centers or special places where gods were worshiped.

Building a royal tomb or pyramid was a major task, so the king sometimes decided that the workers and their families should be housed in a new town. Many children grew up beside the pyramids, and helped with the building as they grew older.

▼ These houses were built on the banks of the Nile. The houses had flat roofs where people slept in summer.

▼ The pyramids and tombs were built further west, in the desert. The Egyptians believed the "Land of the Dead" was in the west.

The countryside

The Egyptians made as much use as possible of the rich soil provided by the Nile mud. They devised a system of irrigation to distribute the water. The *shaduf* was a lever and bucket that took the water from one level to another. The people grew cereals, vegetables, and fruit, and kept animals for food and leather. They kept cows, sheep, goats, pigs, and poultry. They also hunted wild animals on the edges of the desert.

Flax was grown to make linen for clothes, and the papyrus plant gave them writing paper, ropes, boats, sandals, and baskets.

Most people worked on the land. They grew enough to feed themselves and people who did not work on the land. There was a taxation system, but as money was not used until about 525 B.C., people paid in food and goods.

▶ Peasants worked in the fields, growing crops and looking after their animals. On the right is a *shaduf*, used to bring water from a channel up to the land.

The boy-king Tutankhamen

The king of ancient Egypt was called a *pharaoh*. This name comes from the words "per aa," which meant the great house or palace where he lived. The Egyptians believed that the pharaoh was half god and half human and was therefore able to ask the gods for their blessing for himself and for all Egyptians. They believed the pharaoh was very important to Egypt's security and prosperity.

Today, Tutankhamen is the most famous of Egypt's kings because his is the only royal tomb in the Valley of the Kings that has been discovered almost untouched. It was found by the archeologist Howard Carter in 1922 after many years of digging. The king's tomb contained his preserved body, called a *mummy*, a gold head mask, and three golden coffins, as well as clothing, jewelry, perfume, furniture, and games. The Egyptians believed that the dead needed their possessions to use in the next life.

▶ Tutankhamen met with his ministers at the royal court. He wore a double crown to show that he was ruler of Upper (south) and Lower (north) Egypt, and he carried the king's symbols of power, the crook and the flail (whip).

The house

Both rich and poor people built their houses of mud brick and wood. Mud brick was ideal building material in a hot country with little rainfall. In long-established cities and towns where space was limited, houses with two or more floors were built close together. In the new towns, wealthy people built single-level villas surrounded by gardens full of flowers and trees with a lake or pond.

Even the smaller houses often had four rooms with an outside courtyard. The women cooked in pottery ovens built in the courtyard. Inside, the walls were plastered and painted with scenes of animals and the countryside. There were stools, chairs, low tables, beds, and boxes to hold clothes, make-up, jewelry, and household items. Some houses had windows with no glass, and oil lamps for extra lighting.

Ordinary Egyptians prayed at home to gods such as Bes, a jolly dwarf-god, and his wife Tauert, the hippopotamus goddess. People kept statues of some of the gods in their houses.

▼ In this house, the columns were carved in the shape of plants. The windows had no glass, but slats let light into the rooms. The house was the center of many activities such as cooking, eating, sewing, and entertaining.

Daily life

Small children lived with their mother and other female relatives in a special part of the house. The children's clothes were simple and made of linen. Sometimes they had leather or reed sandals, and most wore a bracelet or necklace of beads. It was the custom to shave boys' heads, leaving only one plaited lock. This was cut off when the child reached 12 years.

When their sons were four years old, fathers began to train them in their own profession or trade. Most girls married and looked after the house and their children.

The Egyptians loved their children, but sadly many died at birth or when they were small. Their parents tried to prevent accidents and illness by spells and charms. Many paintings and statues show children as important people in the family group.

▶ Children enjoyed helping in the house and around the village. The weather was hot, so they spent much of the daytime outside. Here, a mother grinds wheat to make bread. Her son holds a cat, the family's favorite pet.

16

Pets and toys

Most Egyptian families had pets. These animals can be found in many of the painted wall-scenes in tombs. The cat was a favorite pet because it killed rats and mice in the house, and the Egyptians believed that the cat-goddess, Bast, protected the home. Some cats may have been specially trained to help their masters when they hunted birds.

► Most families had pet cats, monkeys, or birds. Rich people kept special dogs for hunting. Egyptian children played with many different kinds of toys. They had balls, tops, and pretty dolls with real hair fixed into holes drilled into the head. Some children took part in acrobatics or wrestling competitions.

18

Children had a variety of toys and games. Some of these toys were buried in children's graves so they could play with them in the next world. Other toys have been found in the remains of houses. There were dolls, balls, tops, animal toys, and a board game that resembled checkers. Some children made their own toys, but there were also toy-makers.

Early education

Between the ages of 4 and 14, boys and girls attended school together, where they learned to read, write, and do mathematics. Those who were going to become doctors, lawyers, or scribes (writers) studied the sacred writing called *hieroglyphics*. Students had to copy out stories and religious writings. Some of these exercises survive today. The children also played games, wrestled, and learned to swim.

When boys were 14, they followed their father's trade or profession, which could be working in the fields or joining the craftsmen in government or temple workshops. They could also go on to become doctors, scribes, lawyers, or government officials. Girls usually stayed at home with their mothers to learn how to look after the house.

▶ As the teacher read a story to the class, the children copied it onto pieces of broken pottery or flakes of limestone. Paper, made from papyrus, was too expensive for school work. The children wrote with reed pens and red or black ink.

20

At the market

Each town held a market where people bought food, clothing, and household goods. People needed only simple clothes in such a hot, dry country, but they wore jewelry made of pottery or stone, or sometimes gold, silver, or copper. Rich people covered their heads, as protection against the sun, with wigs made of real hair or grass.

▼ Fruit, vegetables, animals, clothing, pottery vases, and dishes were exchanged at the market, which was held outdoors. Many people brought the food they had grown or the goods they had made, to sell by barter.

Pottery cooking pots and serving dishes were for sale, as well as wooden furniture inlaid with ebony and ivory, or beautiful boxes for make-up.

Egyptians had a lot of gold but not much wood, so they imported cedar wood from Syria. Other goods such as silver, ostrich feathers, ebony, and ivory came from Asia Minor, the Aegean islands, and Nubia, part of present-day Sudan.

23

Dinner time

The rich soil from the Nile's flooding meant that farmers could grow plenty of cereals, vegetables, and fruit. They grew barley, wheat, lentils, cucumbers, beans, leeks, and onions, as well as dates, figs, and grapes. Beef was the Egyptians' favorite meat, but they also ate lamb, pork, goat, fish, duck, and goose.

The basic foods for poorer people were bread, onions, and other vegetables and fruit. Rich people enjoyed much greater variety, including cakes sweetened with honey.

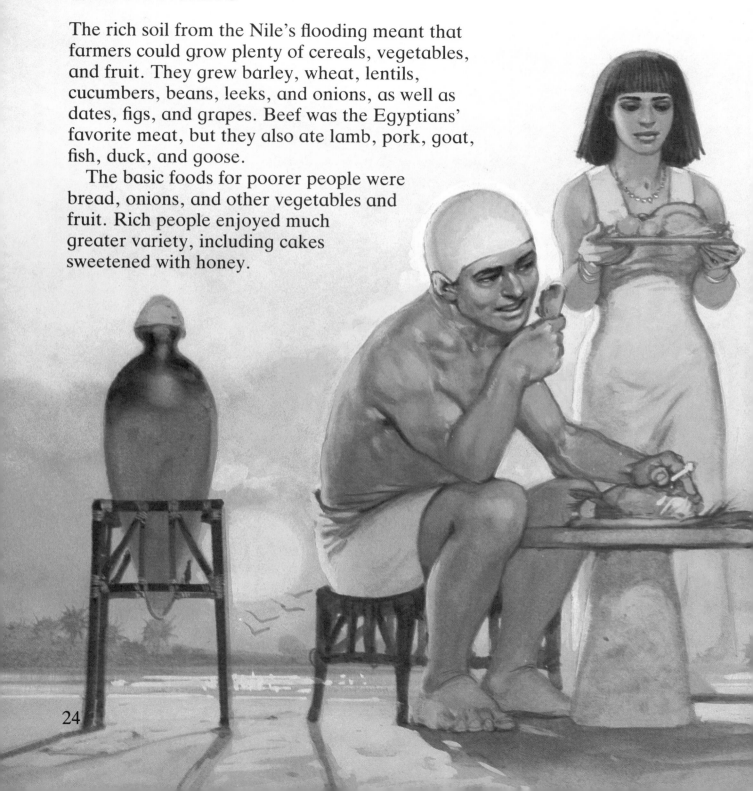

▼ Wealthier people had servants who helped them in the house. Ancient Egyptians did not use knives, forks, or spoons. They ate meat and poultry with their hands, and dipped bread into the other dishes.

Food was cooked in clay ovens in the courtyard and served in pottery dishes at low tables. At midday, some women took a meal to their husbands in the fields and to their children at school.

Priests in the temples served three daily meals to the gods' statues so the gods would help the Egyptians. The food was later removed and divided among priests as payment for their duties.

Visiting the doctor

Many Egyptians became ill from diseases caused by sand and water. Sand in the air caused lung disease and breathing difficulties, and sand in bread wore down people's teeth. Diseases carried by worms in river water caused many problems. The Egyptians also suffered from many illnesses we have today.

The Egyptians probably had the world's earliest medical profession. There were doctors and nurses, and medical students were trained at the temples. Doctors performed operations and created medicines. Some medicines were unpleasant, to frighten away the evil spirit that was thought to cause the illness. Many treatments were recorded in ancient medical documents, with practical remedies as well as magical spells. There was even an attempted cure for the common cold.

▶ Here, a doctor attends to a boy's injured knee. An assistant reads out the ingredients and instructions for making a medicine, while another attendant prepares the treatment.

Childbirth was dangerous, and many mothers and babies died. There were special magical spells designed to protect the newborn and their mothers.

Today, scientists gather information about the ancient Egyptians' diseases, diet, and lifestyle by examining their mummies. They x-ray the mummies, study their blood groups, and examine their body tissue under a microscope.

Getting married

People in ancient Egypt married young. The boys were usually 15 and the girls were about 12. Most people died in their forties, so their lives were short.

Young people chose their partner and wrote love songs to one another. The earliest love songs in the world come from Egypt. Although marriages were not arranged, parents and friends tried to ensure that boys and girls from similar homes and backgrounds met one another.

Egypt today is a very different country. But many of the earlier writings and drawings have been preserved, so we have an excellent idea of what it was like to grow up in such an ancient civilization.

▼ A newly married couple moved their furniture and other possessions into their new home. Neighbors made the couple welcome, with good wishes for a happy marriage.

28

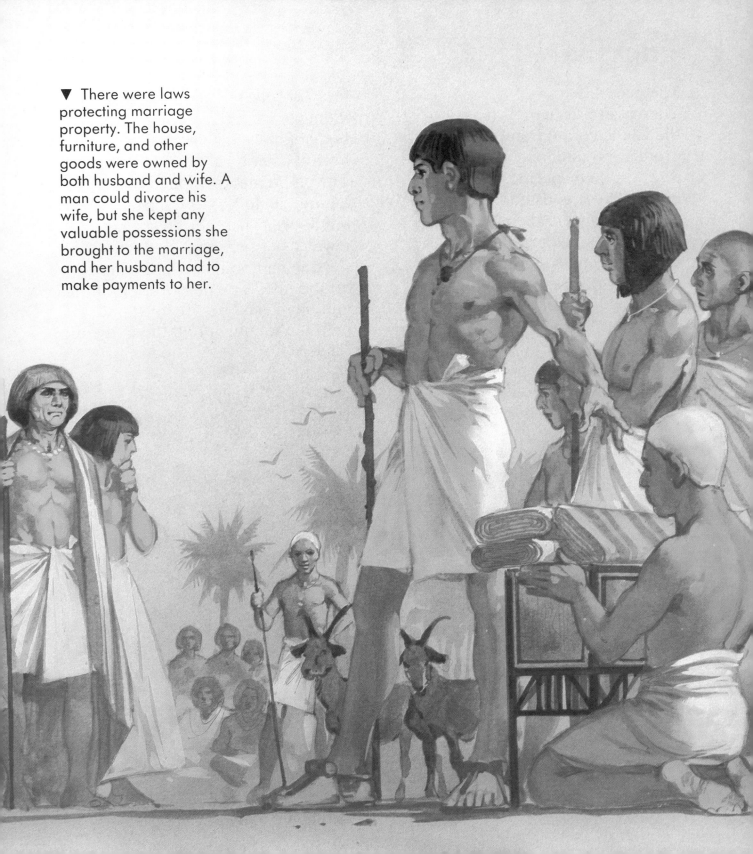

▼ There were laws protecting marriage property. The house, furniture, and other goods were owned by both husband and wife. A man could divorce his wife, but she kept any valuable possessions she brought to the marriage, and her husband had to make payments to her.

Fact file

The gods

There were state gods (in control of the whole country and the king's protectors) and local gods (each powerful in a specific town or area). These gods had temples and priests who were their "servants." There were also priestesses who sang and danced in the temples. Ordinary people prayed to and worshiped household gods in their own homes.

Mummification

After death, the bodies of rich people were mummified. The major body organs (except the heart and kidneys) were removed and the body and organs dried, using natron (a natural mixture of salts). The embalmers wrapped the mummy in layers of linen bandages. They placed special jewelry between the layers, to bring the person good luck in the life after death. The preparation of the mummy lasted for 70 days, and then the family buried the body in a tomb.

▼ Embalmers mummifying a body.

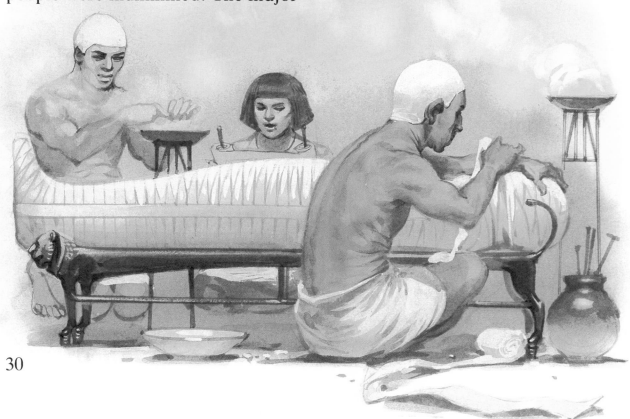

Mummification preserved the body so that the dead person's soul (Ka) could recognize it when the Ka returned to the tomb. The Egyptians believed that the Ka then entered the mummy for a short time, so the dead person could eat the food that his relatives had brought to the tomb.

The pyramids

In some periods, the kings built pyramids as their tombs. These were perhaps intended to look like the sun's rays and to provide a ramp for the dead king to join his father, the sun god. Near the pyramids at Giza, a "sun boat" was found and excavated. The Egyptians may have believed that the dead king used this boat to sail across the sky.

The end of ancient Egyptian civilization

Ancient Egyptian civilization lasted for about 5,000 years, but toward the end, the country was overcome and ruled by foreigners. First came the Assyrians and the Persians, followed by Alexander the Great in 332 B.C. When he died, the country passed to his general, Ptolemy. The Ptolemies then ruled Egypt, ending with Queen Cleopatra VII. The Roman general Octavian finally took Egypt in 30 B.C., and it became a province of the Roman Empire.

Writing

Egyptian language was written in three scripts: hieroglyphics (usually used for texts about history or religious beliefs), hieratic, and demotic (both used for business and everyday matters because they were easier to write). Hieroglyphics were a form of picture writing with about 700 signs. In 1824, a Frenchman, Jean François Champollion, worked out how they should be read, using the Rosetta stone (now in the British Museum, London). This stone had an inscription written in Greek, hieroglyphic, and demotic, honoring King Ptolemy V.

HIEROGLYPHIC					HIERATIC			DEMOTIC
2700–2600 B.C.	2500–2400 B.C.	2000–1800 B.C.	C. 1500 B.C.	500–100 B.C.	C. 1900 B.C.	C. 1300 B.C.	C. 200 B.C.	400–100 B.C.

Index